CAVES

AN UNDERGROUND WONDERLAND

SHENENDEHOWA PUBLIC LIBRARY
47 CLIFTON COUNTRY ROAD
CLIFTON PARK, NEW YORK 12065

JENNY WOOD

Gareth Stevens Children's Books
MILWAUKEE

99457

Wonderworks of Nature:

Caves: An Underground Wonderland
Icebergs: Titans of the Oceans
Storms: Nature's Fury
Volcanoes: Fire from Below

For a free color catalog describing Gareth Stevens' list of high-quality children's books, call 1-800-341-3569 (USA) or 1-800-461-9120 (Canada).

Photographic Credits: p. 5 Planet Earth Pictures; p. 7 (top) Planet Earth Pictures, (bottom) Explorer; p. 8 (top) Bruce Coleman, (bottom) Bruce Coleman; p. 9 (top) GeoScience Features Picture Library, (bottom) Planet Earth Pictures; p. 10 Bruce Coleman; p. 11 Bruce Coleman; p. 12 Planet Earth Pictures; p. 13 (top) Eric & David Hosking, (bottom) Bruce Coleman; p. 14 Survival Anglia Photo Library; p. 15 Eric & David Hosking; pp. 16-17 Planet Earth Pictures; p. 17 (insert) Planet Earth Pictures; p. 18 The Hutchinson Library; p. 19 Bruce Coleman; p. 20 GeoScience Features Picture Library; p. 21 (top) Planet Earth Pictures, (bottom) Bruce Coleman; p. 22 Bruce Coleman; p. 23 Bruce Coleman.

Illustration Credits: pp. 4, 6, 7, 11, 12, 15, 17, 24, 28 Francis Mosley.

Library of Congress Cataloging-in-Publication Data

Wood, Jenny.
    Caves: an underground wonderland / Jenny Wood. — North American ed.
      p. cm. — (Wonderworks of nature)
    Includes index.
    Summary: Text and pictures present the formation, types, inhabitants of, and exploration of caves.
    ISBN 0-8368-0469-4
    1. Caves—Juvenile literature. [1. Caves.] I. Title. II. Series. III. Series: Wood, Jenny. Wonderworks of nature.
GB601.2.W66   1990
508.314'4—dc20   90-55463

This North American edition first published in 1991 by
Gareth Stevens Children's Books
1555 North RiverCenter Drive, Suite 201
Milwaukee, Wisconsin 53212, USA

This U.S. edition copyright © 1991. First published in the United Kingdom by Two-Can Publishing, Ltd. Text copyright © 1990 by Jenny Wood.

All rights reserved. No part of this book may be reproduced or used in any form or by any means without permission in writing from Gareth Stevens, Inc.

Printed in the United States of America

1 2 3 4 5 6 7 8 9 97 96 95 94 93 92 91

CONTENTS

HOW CAVES ARE FORMED

A cave is a natural hollow in the ground which is large enough for a person to enter. Most caves are found in areas of limestone rock.

The process of making a cave takes thousands of years. It starts when surface water trickles down through tiny cracks in the rock. The water contains a gas called carbon dioxide which is absorbed from the air and this forms a mild acid that eats away the limestone. As it travels underground, the water continues to eat away some of the rock, forming passages and caves.

Deep underground is an area known as the **water table**. Here, instead of limestone, there is another type of rock which is already full of water. It can't hold any more, so the water from the surface begins to flow along the line of the water table, forming a small underground river.

The level of the water table may vary over a period of hundreds of years. Each time it does so, the river has to carve out a new route. Air fills the old passages and chambers and, in this way, cave systems are formed.

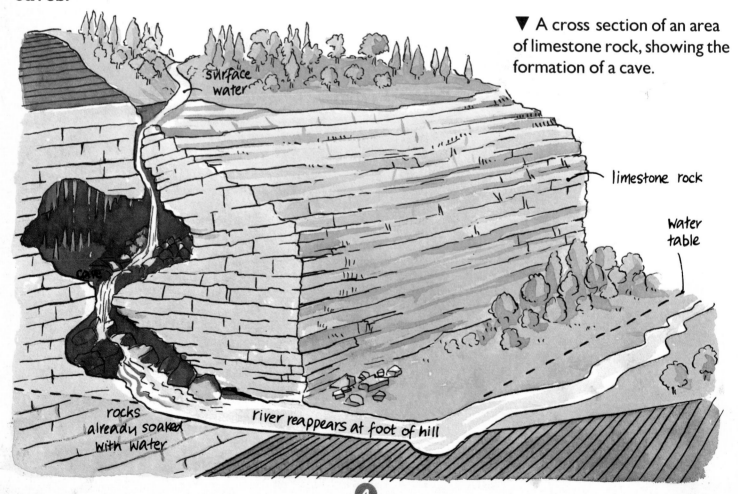

▼ A cross section of an area of limestone rock, showing the formation of a cave.

surface water

limestone rock

water table

CAVE

rocks already soaked with water

river reappears at foot of hill

CAVE SYSTEMS

Over thousands of years, the action of water can create a whole system of caves linked together by a network of tunnels and passageways. These strange underground landscapes are often breathtakingly beautiful and act as reminders of water's ability to carve extraordinary shapes deep underground. Spectacular rock formations appear at every turn. Waterfalls cascade over cliffs. Still underground lakes lie cool and green. Flowing rivers weave their way through the maze. It's little wonder that some of the world's cave systems are now popular tourist attractions.

▼ A cave system might look something like this.

DID YOU KNOW?

● Some cave systems are vast. The world's largest known cave system, for example, the Mammoth-Flint Ridge Cave System in Kentucky, stretches over 300 miles (500 kilometers)!

● The world's largest cave chamber is the Sarawak Chamber in the Gunung Mulu National Park, Sarawak, Malaysia. Its length is 2,300 feet (700 meters), its average width 985 feet (300 m), and nowhere is it less than 230 feet (70 m) high. It is large enough to house 7,500 buses!

● Reseau Jean Bernard in France is the world's deepest known cave. It lies 5,036 feet (1,535 m) below ground.

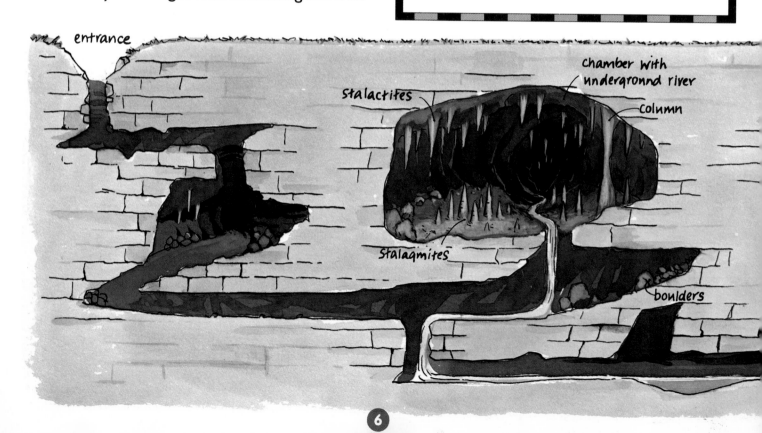

entrance

stalactites

chamber with underground river

column

stalagmites

boulders

▲ Two tunnels lead out of this cave — or is it just one tunnel with two entrances? Only one way to find out . . . !

▼ An underground waterfall.

swallow hole

water-fall

pool

OTHER TYPES OF CAVES

Not all caves are hollowed out of limestone rock. **Lava** tube caves, for example, are formed by red-hot lava flowing from a volcano. As the lava streams down the side of the volcano, its outer surface cools and hardens into rock. Underneath, the lava remains liquid and continues to flow. Eventually it drains away, leaving a hollow tube. These often have very smooth sides and a regular shape. They are usually near the surface and may have many openings in their thin roofs.

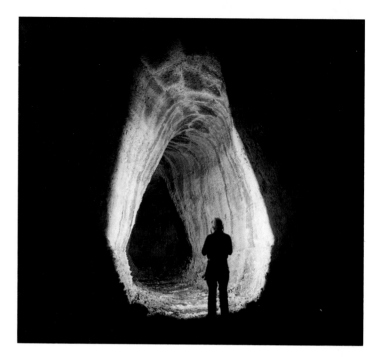

▲ The passage in this lava tube is shaped like a teardrop.

◄ Over many years, the wind and the waves can change the whole appearance of a coastline.

Ice caves usually form inside a **glacier**. As a glacier approaches warmer areas of land, the ice starts to melt. Streams of water form under the ice and these, combined with warm air, hollow out caves.

Shallow coastline caves form along rocky shores as pounding waves and howling winds wear away weak areas of rock.

In some areas of the world, such as the Philippines, there are underwater caves. These were not formed by the sea, but are limestone caves which have sunk under the ocean.

▲ Water from melting ice gushes from the wide entrance of this ice cave at the mouth or "snout" of a glacier in Italy. The water looks thick and white, almost like milk, because it is full of tiny bits of rock and rock dust from the moraine (the debris carried down the mountainside by the glacier and deposited along its edges and around the area of the snout).

◄ A diver explores underwater limestone rock formations.

ROCK FORMATIONS

As water seeps through cracks in limestone, it dissolves a **mineral** called calcite in the rock. Once it has eaten through the limestone and hollowed out a cave, the water continues to dribble down the cave walls. But some water evaporates and a thin layer of calcite is left clinging to the rock. Over thousands of years, the layers of calcite build up. In places they form smooth coverings over the cave walls. Elsewhere, they build up into oddly shaped rock formations or **speleothems**. The best known speleothems are **stalactites** and **stalagmites**. Stalactites hang from the ceiling like icicles. Stalagmites are pillars which rise from the floor. Sometimes a stalagmite and a stalactite join and form a column.

▼ The Carlsbad Caverns in New Mexico contain some of the finest rock formations in the world.

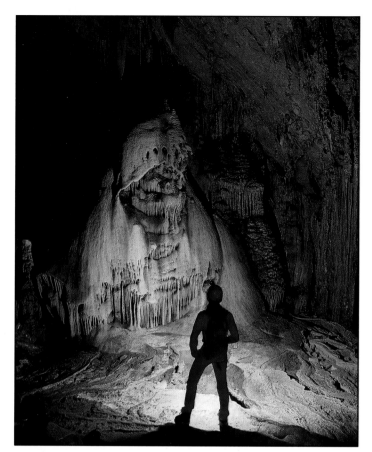

▲ This truly awesome stalagmite is known as "The Klansman."

MAKE YOUR OWN STALACTITES AND STALAGMITES

You will need:
- a piece of thick yarn
- a saucer
- two jam jars
- washing soda (sodium carbonate)

1 Fill the jam jars with warm water. Dissolve as much washing soda as you can in each, a little at a time. Arrange the jars side by side, with the saucer in between.

DID YOU KNOW?

● The longest free-hanging stalactite in the world is thought to be one of 23 feet (7 m) in a cave in County Clare, Ireland.

● The tallest known stalagmite in the world is La Grande Stalagmite in the cave of Aven Armand in France. It is 98 feet (29 m) tall!

● The tallest known cave column in the world is the Flying Dragon Pillar in the Nine Dragons Cave in China. It is 128 feet (39 m) tall!

2 Arrange the yarn so that each end is in one of the jam jars and the middle is hanging over the saucer.

3 Put one crystal of washing soda on the saucer and leave the jars for several days. The water and washing soda solution in the jars will drip on to the crystal in the saucer, forming a column.

CAVE ANIMALS

Almost all caves are cold, damp, and dark. It is unusual for sunlight to reach farther than a small area at the entrance. Yet several types of animals live in caves. Some go in only to rest or to find shelter from the weather, but others spend all their lives there. They feed either on the remains of plants which are carried down from the surface of the land by underground streams, or on each other.

▼ A huntsman spider goes in search of a juicy meal. Most hunting spiders have good eyesight, and can see their prey from a distance.

DID YOU KNOW?

● Inside the Niah Caves in Sarawak, Malaysia, thousands of birds called cave swiftlets roost and nest. Their cup-shaped nests, made from saliva, are edible and the local people collect and sell them. The nests are used to make "bird's nest soup," which is considered a great delicacy in many countries around the world. The people have to build a simple type of scaffolding from bamboo poles, so that they can climb up and reach the nests which are right at the tops of the caves.

▶ Several species of bear, including the black bear and the fearsome grizzly, hibernate in caves during the long, cold winter.

Caves can usually be divided into three "zones." At the entrance of the cave is the "light zone," where sunlight falls. Here you will find green plants such as ferns. Further in is the "twilight zone," where creatures such as bats roost in the dim light. Deep inside the cave is the "dark zone." Many of the animals who live here are white – there is no need for bright skin colors, nor is there any sunlight to affect the color of their skin. Some are also blind. In the darkness of the cave, they have no need for sight. Instead, they have highly developed senses of sound and touch that help them travel through the cave and find food.

▲ The rock hyrax is found in Africa and parts of Asia. It spends much of each day basking in the sun, but runs for cover at any hint of danger.

INTO THE BAT CAVE

Bats like caves and often live in huge colonies. They sleep during the day, hanging from the cave roof, then at dusk they leave the cave for their feeding grounds. Bats are almost blind, but are able to fly safely through the darkness thanks to their highly developed sense of hearing. They use a system of **echo-location**, which works a lot like **radar**. They send out continuous high-pitched sounds, too high-pitched for humans to hear. By listening to the echoes of these sounds bouncing back from obstacles in their path, they can follow a safe route.

In some caves in New Zealand, tiny creatures called glowworms cling to the walls and ceiling. The New Zealand glowworm is the **larva** of a kind of gnat, and its back end gives off light. For food, glowworms spin long, sticky threads to trap flying insects. When enough insects have been caught, the glowworms reel in their threads as if they were fishing lines.

▶ Feeding time! A Greater Horseshoe bat emerges from its cave.

▼ Glowworms twinkle in the darkness.

The red lines represent the high-pitched sounds which a bat sends out. When these sound waves hit an object (like an insect), echoes (the blue lines) bounce back toward the bat, telling it exactly where the object is.

CAVE PAINTING

Over thirty thousand years ago, people began to engrave and paint on cave walls. These early artists mixed their own paints using substances such as charcoal, clay, plant juices, and animal blood. They painted with four basic colors – black, white, red, and yellow. Sometimes the paint was simply rubbed onto the surface of the rock, but simple brushes made of animal hair or vegetable fibers were also used. Hollowed-out bones were often used to blow the paint onto the rock.

Most of these early cave paintings were of animals. Historians now believe that the paintings were used during special ceremonies which early people performed to help them succeed in hunting the animal or animals pictured.

▼ These patterns may have been an early type of calendar or map.

DID YOU KNOW?

● The caves at Lascaux in France had to be closed to the public because of the damage caused to the paintings by the breath from the thousands of tourists! A complete replica of the caves, including the paintings, has now been built alongside the original.

● Many cave paintings have been found high up on cave walls and ceilings. The artists must have used ropes, or simple ladders or scaffolding made from tree trunks, to help them reach.

▶ Hundreds of cave painting sites have now been discovered all over the world. This painting was found in Zimbabwe.

CAVE DWELLERS

About 100,000 years ago most of Europe was in the grip of an Ice Age. The Neanderthal people who lived at that time used caves as homes. They usually settled near the entrances to the caves, where they had both light and shelter.

We know quite a lot about these early people from the remains of stone and bone tools found in their caves. It seems that Neanderthals were excellent hunters who killed large woolly **mammoths** and rhinos, as well as reindeer and bison. They were the first people to bury their dead.

Traces of earlier cave dwellers have been found in southern France and near Beijing in China. There, prehistoric people occupied caves between 500,000 and 250,000 years ago.

But caves have never been very popular dwellings. Today, only a few cave dwellers can be found in parts of Africa, Asia, Europe, and the Near East.

▶ The Goreme Valley in Turkey is riddled with caves which have been dug out over thousands of years.

▼ The Ajanta Caves in India were hollowed out of granite cliffs more than 1,300 years ago.

EXPLORING CAVES

In 1881 a man called Tom Bingham was hunting deer in the Black Hills of South Dakota. Suddenly he heard a strange whistling sound coming from a clump of brush. When he investigated, he discovered a cave entrance! The cave was later named Wind Cave because of the strong currents of wind which blow alternately in and out of its mouth.

Today, cavers use more scientific methods when searching for new caves. They start by looking at **geological maps** for clues. Streams which suddenly disappear, or large hollows which should contain lakes but don't, point to the existence of underground tunnels into which water is draining.

Fluorescent dyes can be poured into a stream so that its underground

▼ Inflatable dinghies are used for crossing wide lakes and rivers.

DID YOU KNOW?

● The scientific study of caves is called **speleology** and the people who study caves are known as **speleologists**.

● Cavers are also called **spelunkers**, and the sport is known as **spelunking**. In Britain they are called **potholers**.

◄ Sea caves, like this coral cave, can be very beautiful.

▼ The entrance to this cave system is a sheer drop of about 55 feet (17 m)!

course can be traced. Once a system has been traced, the rest is up to the cavers.

Caving is a popular and exciting sport, though it can be dangerous. Cavers always explore in groups, and they carry sturdy ropes and other climbing gear. They wear hard hats and tough, heavy clothing as protection against the jagged rocks and dripping water. Sometimes they need to use diving equipment.

Cavers spend a lot of time on their hands and knees crawling through low passages, or wriggling through awkward gaps. Sometimes they have to squirm through a "squeeze" where the tunnel is just big enough for their bodies!

SCIENCE AT WORK

Caves provide historians and scientists who are interested in the development of human beings with an enormous amount of information about prehistoric cave dwellers and their way of life. As well as studying the bones and many other kinds of litter which are found in caves, scientists also study the layers of soil on a cave floor. The materials which make up each layer give clues as to what the climate was like at a particular time.

Scientists are then able to build up a picture of the kind of countryside that prehistoric humans lived in and the kinds of plants and animals which thrived there.

▼ Fossils are the preserved remains of prehistoric plants or animals. They tell us the story of the earth, and show us how animals and plants have changed and developed. Most fossils are found in rock, although some have been found in ice, tar, and hardened tree sap called amber.

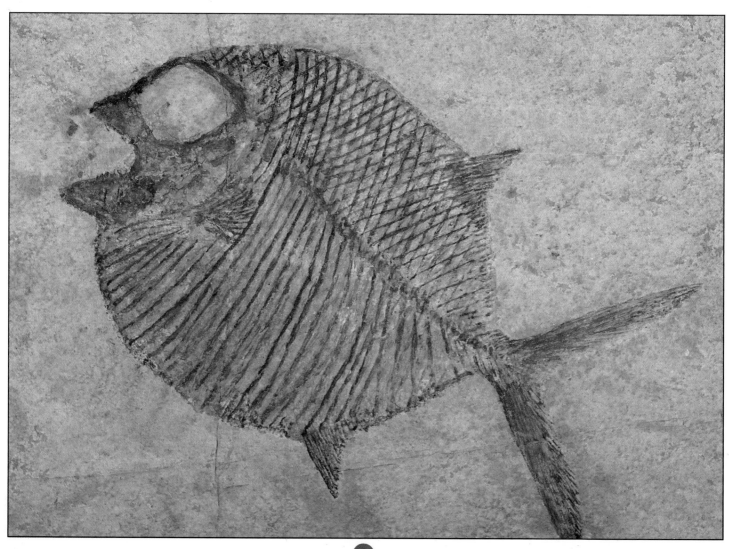

Another group of scientists who are interested in caves are **geologists**. Geologists study caves, rocks, soils, mountains, rivers, oceans, and other parts of the earth. Many of them want to find out about the history of the earth and how it has changed over millions of years. The layers of rock in the earth's crust and the **fossils** found in them provide clues.

Geologists also explore the earth for coal, oil, gas, uranium, and other materials that supply energy. They

▲ Most gold used today is found deep underground. Scientists believe that gold is deposited from gases and liquids rising from beneath the earth's surface. These gases and liquids travel toward the surface through cracks in the crust, and are deposited in veins in the rock. The mining of gold is now an important industry.

look for underground deposits of metals such as copper, gold, iron, lead, silver, and tin. And they try to find sources of precious stones such as diamonds and emeralds.

AN AMAZING DISCOVERY

It was a warm Sunday afternoon in September 1940. Four friends, Marcel Ravidat, Jacques Marsal, Georges Agnel, and Simon Coencas, were exploring the woods on a hill overlooking the town of Montignac in southwest France.

Suddenly Marcel shouted to his friends.

"Come and look at this!"

Hearing the note of excitement in his voice, the three other boys ran to see what he had found. There between the roots of a dead tree was a dark, deep hole.

Jacques peered down into the darkness. "It looks as if it goes right down into the bowels of the earth."

The strange hole did seem to have no end. It was as if, down under the dead tree, there was a hollow bubble of dark nothingness.

"Perhaps it's the secret underground passage which leads to Lascaux Manor," said Georges. "You know, the one Monsieur Laval was telling us about at school."

"That would be a find!" said Simon. For years people had talked about this secret passage, but no one had ever found it.

"Come on then," urged Marcel. "What are we waiting for? Let's explore."

"No," said Simon, "not now. It'll be dark soon and there'll be trouble if we're not home for dinner. Let's do this properly. We should take a whole afternoon and we'll need a light and some ropes."

"You're right, " said Jacques. "Why don't we come back on Thursday? We're off school that afternoon."

"OK then," agreed Marcel, although he didn't know how he would be able to wait four whole days.

But Thursday came soon enough. The boys met by the dead tree with a homemade oil lamp, a few bits of rope, and a knife. They set to work clearing away the undergrowth from around the hole.

"How deep do you think it is?" asked Georges, peering down into the blackness.

"No idea," replied Simon. "Why don't we try throwing a few stones into it?

We might be able to guess the depth by listening to the stones falling."

The stones fell and rolled for a long time.

"It must be very deep," said Simon. "Perhaps we shouldn't go down."

"We'll just have to be careful," said Jacques. "Now come on, let's stop wasting time!"

One by one the boys squeezed through. They slid and tumbled down and down. At last they stopped, none the worse for the fall, at the bottom of the hole. Even the oil lamp had survived its journey.

In the lamp's dim light, the boys could see that they were in a huge underground chamber. The walls seemed to be covered with lines and dots.

"Turn up the lamp and hold it higher," said Georges. "I want to get a better look at these walls." His voice echoed through the cave.

Jacques did as he was asked. As the lamp began to light up the cave, the lines and spots seemed to grow into the shapes of bulls and deer. The walls were covered with paintings!

"These paintings must have been made by cavemen thousands of years ago."

"And no one has seen them for thousands of years!" added Simon.

It had taken them quite some time to get into the cave and already the light from the entrance was growing dim.

"We should really tell someone about this," said Simon.

"Not yet," Marcel replied decidedly. "I want to see it all before we let anyone else know. I think we should come back tomorrow and really explore."

So the next day, the boys returned to their secret place. This time they found a gallery leading off the main chamber and a shaft. The walls of both were covered with paintings.

Later that day, the boys decided to tell Monsieur Laval, their schoolteacher, about their great find. He realized at once that, if the boys' story was true, they had stumbled upon what might be one of the most important sites of prehistoric painting ever discovered. But he decided to go and look for himself, just to make sure before telling anyone else.

Six days later, after the boys had cleared and widened the hole still further, the schoolmaster entered the cave. As soon as he saw the paintings he knew that the boys had been right. This was an extraordinary find.

The news of Lascaux Cave spread fast. Historians and tourists were soon flocking to Montignac to see the paintings. Today the ancient paintings have begun to suffer from exposure to the air, so the climate in the cave is carefully controlled. Scientists and historians are at work there, trying to find out more about the paintings and the people who painted them.

If you are ever lucky enough to be shown around Lascaux Cave, your guide could be none other than Jacques Marsal, one of the boys who first stumbled on the hole between the roots of a dead tree all those years ago!

TRUE OR FALSE?

Which of these facts are true and which ones are false?
If you have read this book carefully, you will know the answers.

1 Most caves are found in areas of hard rock called granite.

2 Rock formations are known as speleothems.

3 A rock hyrax is another name for a potholer.

4 Caves can provide historians with lots of information about how prehistoric people lived.

5 The world's largest known cave system is in France.

6 Stalactites are pillar-like rock formations which rise from the floor of a cave.

7 Many animals who live deep inside caves are white because there is no sunlight to affect the color of their skin.

8 Lava tube caves often have very smooth sides and a regular shape.

9 Most early cave paintings were of people.

10 "Bird's nest soup" is made from the nests of birds called cave swiftlets.

11 Bats have a special system of hearing known as echo-location.

12 Ice caves usually form underwater.

13 The words spelunking, potholing, and caving are all used to describe the sport of exploring caves.

Answers: 1 False; 2 True; 3 False; 4 True; 5 False; 6 False; 7 True; 8 True; 9 False; 10 True; 11 True; 12 False; 13 True.

GLOSSARY

Echo-location is the name given to the way in which bats, who are almost blind, find out the position of obstacles in their path. When the high-pitched sounds a bat sends out hit an object, echoes of these sounds bounce back toward the bat. The bat is then able to tell exactly where the object is and move round it.

Fossils are the preserved remains of prehistoric plants or animals. Most are found in rock. Although soft and hard parts of a creature can be preserved, sometimes all that is left is a print of its shape or feet.

Fluorescent dyes are used by cavers when exploring cave systems. They are poured into streams or rivers which disappear underground. The light given off by the dyes allows the cavers to trace the underground route of the water, and to discover the place where the water reappears on the surface.

Geological maps show the different types of rock found in a particular area, as well as the area's physical features.

Geologist is a scientist who studies the rocks and other substances which make up the earth's crust (surface layer).

Glacier is the name given to a slowly moving river of ice.

Larva is the grub or caterpillar form of an insect.

Lava is the name given to magma (hot, liquid rock found inside the earth in the layer called the mantle) when it escapes onto the earth's surface.

Mammoth is a type of hairy elephant which lived in prehistoric times.

Mineral is the general name given to any substance (other than a vegetable substance) which can be dug from the ground. Coal, oil, and iron are minerals, for example.

Potholing is the British word for the sport of exploring caves and underground passages. A person who follows this sport is known as a potholer.

Radar is a type of radio system which detects solid objects that come within its range. It works in a similar way to the system of echo-location used by bats. The radio waves from the radar equipment bounce back when they come into contact with a solid object, and the position of the object is then shown on a computer screen. Radar is used by sailors and by pilots.

Speleology is the scientific study of caves. Scientists who study caves are known as speleologists.

Speleothem is the scientific name for an unusually shaped rock formation. Speleothems are formed over thousands of years from layers of a mineral called calcite which build up on the walls and/or floor and/or ceiling of a cave.

Spelunking is the American word for potholing. A person who follows the sport of spelunking is known as a spelunker.

Stalactites are speleothems. They hang down from the ceiling of a cave.

Stalagmites are speleothems. They build up from the floor of a cave.

Swallow hole, also known as a pothole, is a tunnel or shaft that leads straight down through a section of limestone rock. It is formed by water wearing away the rock over many years.

Water table is the upper surface of an area of rock that is permanently soaked with water and so can hold no more.

INDEX